my bad parent

TROY OSINOFF

my bad parent

DO AS I SAY,
NOT AS I DID

A PERIGEE BOOK

A PERIGEE BOOK
Published by the Penguin Group
Penguin Group (USA) Inc.
375 Hudson Street, New York, New York 10014, USA

Penguin Group (Canada), 90 Eglinton Avenue East, Suite 700, Toronto, Ontario
M4P 2Y3, Canada (a division of Pearson Penguin Canada Inc.) • Penguin Books
Ltd., 80 Strand, London WC2R 0RL, England • Penguin Ireland, 25 St. Stephen's
Green, Dublin 2, Ireland (a division of Penguin Books Ltd.) • Penguin Group (Australia),
707 Collins Street, Melbourne, Victoria 3008, Australia (a division of Pearson
Australia Group Pty. Ltd.) • Penguin Books India Pvt. Ltd., 11 Community Centre,
Panchsheel Park, New Delhi—110 017, India • Penguin Group (NZ), 67 Apollo
Drive, Rosedale, Auckland 0632, New Zealand (a division of Pearson New
Zealand Ltd.) • Penguin Books, Rosebank Office Park, 181 Jan Smuts Avenue,
Parktown North 2193, South Africa • Penguin China, B7 Jaiming Center, 27 East
Third Ring Road North, Chaoyang District, Beijing 100020, China
Penguin Books Ltd., Registered Offices: 80 Strand, London WC2R 0RL, England

While the author has made every effort to provide accurate telephone
numbers, Internet addresses, and other contact information at the time of
publication, neither the publisher nor the author assumes any responsibility
for errors, or for changes that occur after publication. Further, the publisher
does not have any control over and does not assume any responsibility for
author or third-party websites or their content.

We'd like to thank and give credit to the following who generously contributed
their photos: Jessica Jones, Janaye Fentroy, Eric Williams, Adam and Alyssa
De La Serna, Kiera Dixon, Blaire and Max Hilliard, Chris Duval, Noah
Rodenbeek, Christopher Senez, and Mark Gill.

After extensive searches, the sources of the photographs on pages 62, 81, 107, 114,
123, 124, 131, and 136—which can be found on numerous sites on
the Internet—are unknown.

First edition: November 2012

Osinoff, Troy.
My bad parent : do as I say, not as I did / Troy Osinoff.—1st ed.
p. cm.
ISBN 978-0-399-16160-5
1. Parenting—Humor. 2. Parenthood—Humor. I. Title.
PN6231.P2085   2012
818'.607—dc23   2012030138

Most Perigee books are available at special quantity discounts for bulk purchases for
sales promotions, premiums, fund-raising, or educational use. Special books, or book
excerpts, can also be created to fit specific needs. For details, write: Special Markets,
Penguin Group (USA) Inc., 375 Hudson Street, New York, New York 10014.

CONTENTS

Introduction   vii

①
Let's Talk About Sex, um, Baby   1

②
Child Transport Made Complicated   21

③
Child Storage Tips   35

④
Creative Potty Training   55

(5)

Happy Fun Time with Baby   65

(6)

Let's Play Dress-Up!   87

(7)

Self-Defense: The Shame Neutralizer   105

(8)

Kids + Kegs = Kigs!™   125

(9)

PSA: Just Say No to Bath Salts   145

Photo Credits   163

INTRODUCTION

LONG AGO, AT A MCDONALD'S NOT VERY FAR AWAY...

I was sitting in the outdoor section of a McDonald's, just eating my McSammich like any self-disrespecting American, when I saw something that made me stop mid-chew. You know those harnesses some people put on their kids? The kind with the retractable leash? Maybe you haven't seen this. But that's what it is: a harness and leash, but instead of being attached to, say, a dog or the Gimp from *Pulp Fiction*, the contraption is locked onto a kid, and the parent just drags the kid around like a house pet.

I suppose child leashes are useful. It's a dangerous world out there. You don't want to lose track of your kid. The problem about the kid I saw at the Mickey D's was that he was totally into walking and crawling around and exploring with wide eyes this amazing new world of his and, you know, being a kid. The nerve, right? Somebody put some drugs in this brat. Definitely something wrong with him.

Anyway, the mom and dad had locked their end of the leash onto one leg of their picnic table, and the leash was getting tangled on all the legs as the kid crawled in and out and around them. I watched until the kid was so tangled up that he couldn't even move. He didn't actually seem too pissed off about it. In fact, it seemed like he was used to it. He wasn't crying or anything, just calmly lying there in a tangled mess like a fresh catch, patiently awaiting freedom as Mom and Dad contentedly stuffed Frankenfood into their greasy faces.

Is this normal? I thought. *I mean really?*

It turns out that whole child-leash thing might not be normal, per se, but it is common.

But that was nothing. I acquired pictures of parents doing all kinds of crazy things—stuff that's not exactly abuse but sure makes you wonder where our species is headed.

A really pissed-off house pet.

Zen and the Art of Child Humiliation.

There's the grinning baby, duct-taped to a wall next to her favorite giant yellow duck; a photo op with a very unhappy girl sitting captive on the crust-ridden lap of someone whom I can only presume is the Crypt Keeper's great-grandmother in her Sunday best; a dad dangling his toddler by the ankles so the toddler can hand-feed some (angry? rabid?) raccoons at what is likely the world's shittiest zoo; a whole boatload of kids doing grown-up things like downing beer and posing with their favorite semiautomatic weapons and chillin' at the strip club . . . The list goes on.

I had stumbled on a heretofore unexplored niche. I was moved—inspired, even. I started throwing these hidden treasures onto a website I dubbed MyBadParent.com, which quickly gained a few thousand loyal visitors. Pretty soon I had readers coming out of the woodwork to submit pictures of questionable child-rearing practices from around the world.

There was no denying it: There's just something universally heartwarming and life-affirming about a kid tied to a window grate, a clueless toddler presented with a dick-shaped cookie on her birthday, or a baby clutching a frothy beer stein with a vacuous baby smile pinned to his cute little baby face.

Making fun of crappy moms and dads has been a rewarding experience for me these last couple of years. In this book, I would like to share with you some of my very favorite bad parents and their hapless genetic inheritors.

At the same time, this book illustrates and explicates as clearly as photographically possible how you too can become the absolute worst parent you can be, should you ever wake up one boozy morning only to discover you've spawned.

I believe it was Mother Teresa, the most famous mother of all, who said:

> If I can completely humiliate just one endearingly dumb-ass parent in this lifetime—and make everybody laugh at that dumb-ass—then it will have all been worth it.

Amen, sister. Let the humiliation begin.

LET'S TALK ABOUT SEX, UM, BABY

IT ALL BEGINS WITH A LOOK. You know the look. She looks at him, he looks at her gigantic pregnant belly, they both look at the hard liquor, and boom: Six days later, a brand-new family of unknown paternity is staring at each other and silently asking, *"How the hell...?"*

How the hell, indeed. That's the question your child will be asking you when he grows old enough to notice he's obviously not from the same planet as you are—and other potentially difficult questions. To wit:

Where did I come from?
Why are the people on TV putting their faces
    together?

Why is that grown woman all naked and twirling around a fireman pole, and why are you throwing my diaper money at her?

When such questions start flying, this chapter will get you out of the weeds.

The opposite of how a baby shows up to your party.

He'll always remember what color marker she was wearing the first day he threw up on her.

"There is no stork, silly.
We have the postal service now."

A lot easier than having The Talk.

Hidden inside:
GOODNIGHT MOON.

Dumbo, lost and desperate,
joins a traveling condom sales team.

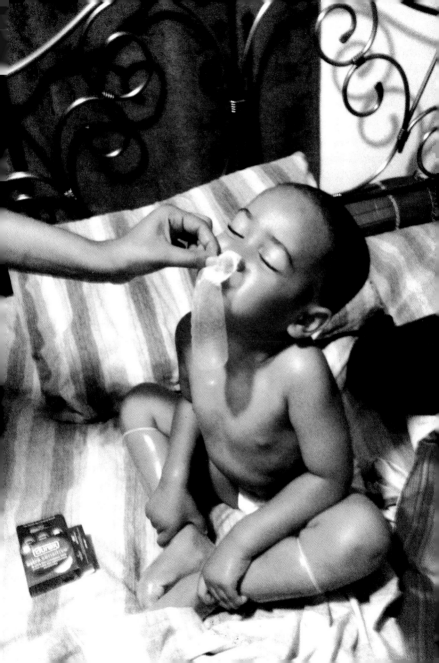

"Wait, wait, I think I can make it into the shape of a child tax credit!"

"This one is only $11.99, as it's a little bent."

"Mom! Dad! I am SHOCKED! I DEMAND the strawberry syrup."

Bring Your Child to Work Day.

P.P.S. Your dinner is a steaming pile of unpleasant surprises. Happy screwing!

Son,

I know you have grown up now, and I'm proud of you. When Ashley comes over tonight, if things get serious, make sure you are SAFE!

Use this!
→

P.S. Your dinner is in the fridge honey.

Love Mom

X-tremely dizzy fetus.

Christening Her Majesty's Ship
THE ROYAL ACCIDENT.

Mothers everywhere
rejoiced when the
medical establishment
announced wine
actually turns your
fetus into a genius.

How I REALLY Met Your Mother . . .

. . . and Your "Aunt."

2

CHILD TRANSPORT MADE COMPLICATED

SOON AFTER YOUR BABY LEAVES THE WOMB, HE BECOMES KIND OF A USELESS PAIN IN THE ASS: YOU HAVE TO TOTE HIM AROUND. That requires gas money or bicycle money or a suitcase, and who can afford that? It sucks and it's not fair. But sometimes life just sells you a lemon, and you have to make pissy, overpriced lemonade out of it. Or however the metaphor goes. Think positive-ish, is all I'm saying.

The uplifting news is there is no shortage of ways to get your child from point A to the strip club. The bad parents in this chapter have selflessly donated their incompetent example to show you the right ways to jerry-rig a front-seat redneck car seat, make a motorcycle baby sandwich using Mom and Dad as the bread, and deal with that one whiny little girl who can't man up to being stuffed like a sack of potatoes in the rear window well of a two-door sedan.

Junk in the trunk.

Seat belts are for sissy-boys.

Front seat, back seat, tomayto, tomahto.

MY BAD PARENT

It's cool as long as you brake kind of slowly.

Out of frame to right:
12-foot jump.

Not seen: the rest of the water cooler on the other side.

"Give Daddy a turn, honey."

"Try to keep it below 35!"

This is just wrong. Isn't there supposed to be an antenna there?

"Dad, when do WE get to have a water cooler?"

"Hang on, boy! Just three more laps to go!"

Is this a punishment or a reward?
Place your bets.

American ingenuity at work.

"Oh my god! He'd better be careful or he's going to bend that poster board."

3

CHILD STORAGE TIPS

SCREW IT. You're tired of driving your kid everywhere. Soccer practice this, emergency medical procedure that, *blah, blah, blah*. Who needs it? Not you, aspiring bad parent. Not you. Wouldn't it be nice if you could just stow your little bundle of joylessness like a carry-on bag—anywhere, anytime, so you can take off and properly enjoy your precious little time on this earth playing video games? Don't you think you deserve that?

Or maybe you want to keep your kid with you, but your kid is sticky and you don't want to touch her.

I've got you covered. The bad parents in this chapter are live child storage *professionals*. They know how to sling a roll of duct tape, you know what I mean? And have you ever considered the limitless child storage possibilities of a shopping cart? These parents have. Watch and learn.

How Mr. T got his 'tude.

"Now . . . where did I put that 'baby' thing?"

"La Sierra AGAIN?"

Ladies and gentlemen, the collapsible
Stow-a-Baby! APPLAUSE.

Wilsons Leather: Made from Genuine Babies!

MY BAD PARENT

As long as no one starts throwing darts, what's the problem here?

Mario Kart.

These things tend to crop up if you don't use antibacterial soap on your floors.

MY BAD PARENT

"As long as she doesn't wake up, we're cool."

"Boy howdy, these magnetically attached
baby backpacks are swell!"

The muffled cries of his four siblings grew
fainter as the day wore on.

"Hang tight, sweetie.
We'll be back after the weekend."

"Honey, there was a fire sale at the orphanage!"

Shopping cart barnacle.

Future Cirque du Soleil star.

Sir, you can't sell that here.
You'll need to go to aisle 7.

MY BAD PARENT

4

CREATIVE POTTY
TRAINING

SHIT. That's what we're dealing with here. Load after load of it. And piss. Oh, you thought I was going to mince words? You must have skipped the first three grisly chapters and headed straight for this one—the one with "potty" in the title. What are you, some kind of human-waste aficionado, some Rabelaisian scatologist?

That's OK. Be yourself. We're practically family now. And family doesn't let family not cover the finer points of weaning your children off the diaper and onto the crapper, or stuck in the toilet seat cover, or just sitting in a yellow bucket and letting it all go. All of these options are close enough to ideal.

Consider this chapter your complete guide to bad potty training. I've even included some creative ways to treat child constipation!

"See, son, you wanna aim for the . . . dammit. I keep forgetting God cursed me with a GIRL."

When push comes to shove, you roll them sonsabitches into the cat box aisle.

Constructive potty training feedback.

9.4, 9.4, 9.6! 9.4, 9.3, and a massive 9.9! What an upset!

Intestines are like toothpaste tubes: always squeeze from the FAR end.

If the kid is having trouble going to the bathroom, this ought to clear the pipes in 3 . . . 2 . . .

"Oh my God, he's bleeding from the head! Wait, no. He's fine. Just move him away from the fake grass. It's new."

Up until now, his worst recurring nightmare was getting eaten by a toilet. Now it's a carnivorous camera.

5

HAPPY FUN TIME
WITH BABY

BAD PARENTING ISN'T ALL WORK. Kids can be a blast. Sometimes your children will surprise you with their shameless zest for life, and just transport you from the everyday drudgery of dealing pot and blowing mad cash on some fine-ass hoes.

Playground slides are cool, too, though. You can push your baby down one as a legal and safe form of revenge, if you want. The kid might not like it, but the look on his face will be priceless. Just find something you like to do, and share it with your child. Are you artistic? Have your child draw a picture in homage to her favorite evil deity. If you're musical, try using your dog and your newborn son as a pair of orchestral cymbals. Hard up for cash? Homeless? Chill out with your kid in the electronics section at the department store and catch some football.

Think you can out-fun these parents?

Mary Lou Retton's dirty little secret of a son.

"Let me know when you're done changing the oil, honey."

"Yawn. Feed me a Dorito through my Dorito hole, then bear left. Your MILITARY left."

"That's right . . . nice and easy . . .
NOW GRAB HIM!"

MY BAD PARENT

He had wowed crowds at the Ring Toss to win
the top prize: a human child . . .
but now what?

"Woooo, Daddy! This is rad! I'm having so much fun! I— zzzzz . . ."

MY BAD PARENT

A second later he slams them together like two garbage can lids.

Most fun this kid has seen in weeks.

"Don't say I never did anything for you."

This was the corrected version.

How to Infect Your Child
with 47 Different Forms
of Bubonic Plague in One
Easy Step.

Kids and parents alike detested
the ill-conceived Sea of Gasoline.

Setup for the world's most
committed planking ever.

And as he reached the bottom, he came face-to-face with the world's largest Brussels sprout.

"Anyone else smell that?"

"Daddy's going to hide now! Come find Daddy!
HEH HEH HEH . . ."

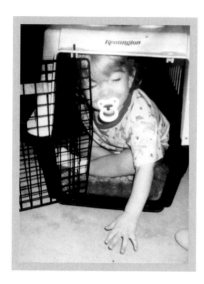

Kid Kennel Rugs:
Made from
Genuine Dog Fur,
for Long-Lasting
Comfort™

Ten seconds earlier:
"Can I have a chain
saw?" "Ho ho no."

13787

A rousing game of Find Where Mommy Hid
Your Clothes.

As close to boogieboarding as this kid will ever get.

It's a keeper!

Rollback on babies.

MY BAD PARENT

6

LET'S PLAY DRESS-UP!

DRESS-UP IS AN AGE-OLD PARENT-CHILD ACTIVITY, UNIVERSAL ACROSS ALL CULTURES THROUGHOUT HISTORY. Boys and girls alike enjoy playing dress-up, and you will, too, if you put your mind to the vodka. Not sure how to play? Pour yourself another shot. You'll remember.

As with all of the other parent-child activities illustrated in this book, be creative! Don't just do the usual cowboy/cowgirl, prince/princess, ninja/terrorist/ sex offender dress-up routines. All families do those.

Set yourself apart. Be unique—just like the parents who inflicted their creative visions on the children in this chapter. Dress-up, when played with that unmistakable *My Bad Parent* pizzazz, excites the imagination and leaves scars that will last a lifetime.

MY BAD PARENT

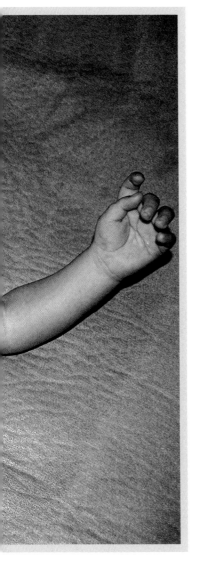

"You might know me from such photos as DICK COOKIE and ALL HAIL SATAN."

Tales from the Crib.

MY BAD PARENT

Commander Suffocate of Starship Grocery Cart discovers Planet Pass-Out.

MY BAD PARENT

Rescue crews bravely fly out to investigate Commander Suffocate's sudden radio silence.

"Get the Vaseline."

1972: Janet plots her infamous wardrobe malfunction.

Dress-up from the ground up, for the low price of 50 cents.

MY BAD PARENT

"So, you're all going as hobos, then?"

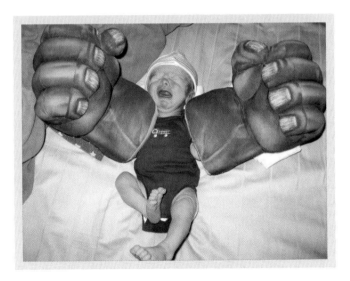

Licensed merchandise make Hulk Baby angry.

Five seconds of hilarity.
Twelve years of therapy.

It's that new NONtoxic form of toxic ink.

MY BAD PARENT

Keith Haring's cheap hired canvas.

MY BAD PARENT

7

SELF-DEFENSE: THE
SHAME NEUTRALIZER

AS YOUR CHILD AGES, HIS GROWING OBSESSION WITH PLAYING DRESS-UP IS INEVITABLY GOING TO GET HIS ASS KICKED. Some bigoted, unfair bully at school is going to take one look at the diaper on your child's head and the permanent tattoo of the Vagisil logo on his face, and just start beating him with a tennis racket. It happens to every child.

After your own laughter wears off, you might feel a little ashamed that your own flesh and blood lost a fight. That's why you need to teach your kid some basic self-defense, regardless of whether your child is a girl, a boy, or a little of both. Real bad parents know all the best ways to teach a child to destroy any opponent. It's not about babying your baby—teaching him prancy little forms, blathering on about "honor," or any of that other rot they spout down at the karate dojo. It's about literally throwing your child in with the snakes and lions and letting him shoot it out.

In teaching your child to defend himself, remember the old rule of thumb: If you don't kill them while they're young, they'll never learn.

"Aww, look, honey. They're making friends."

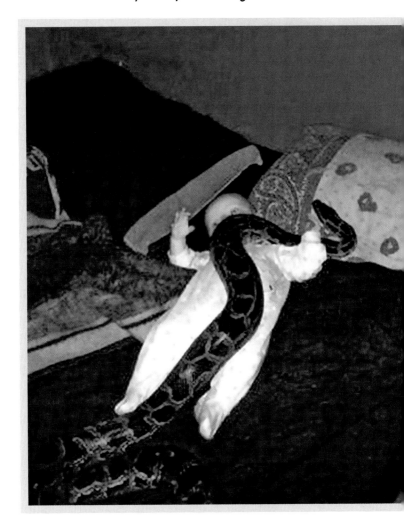

"Escape that and you can have dinner, grasshopper."

Duct Tape Wars, Level 2.

Ha ha ha, oh, boys. Always literally murdering each other. Let them be.

I said NO jalapeños, you moron.
I'll bet you didn't even graduate high school.

Sustained Direct Sunlight Exposure Training.
Bonus: Fry an egg on him and let him watch
you eat it!

"Go show your sister who Daddy's favorite is."

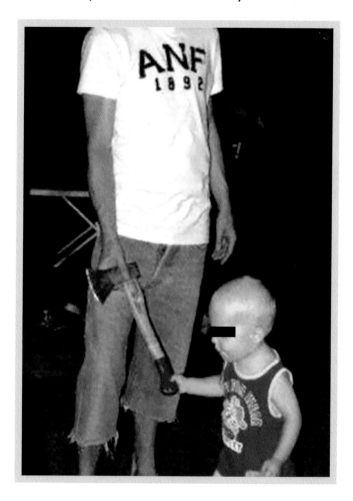

That's more like it. I only eat food grown by good, decent, white children.

Jake's hilarious antics always kept the Mumford family in good spirits.

Children 1, Oscar the Grouch 0.

If he wasn't such a wuss, it could have been a sweet picture.

MY BAD PARENT

"Quick! Take the picture before she loses consciousness!"

"Rock-a-bye Bessie, on the gun rack—SHUT UP, Junior. Bessie needs her sleep."

MY BAD PARENT

Locked, loaded, and lovable.

Timmy always loved shooting himself in the mouth as a way to make his little sister chuckle.

MY BAD PARENT

8

KIDS + KEGS = KIGS!™

ACCORDING TO THE LATEST MEDICAL FINDINGS I FOUND INSIDE MY MIND, BEER IS THE MOST EFFECTIVE WAY TO TREAT BORING-ASS KIDS LIKE YOURS. This corroborates something my dear mother says to me all the time: "Troy, stop your boring-ass whining and chug, chug, chug . . ."

The bad parents in the following photos demonstrate in full color the right way and the wrong way to do keg stands with your child. Get tips on the right size beer bong—and regular old bong—to coach your kids with. See examples of some seriously talented children doing the One-Handed Bud, the Two-Handed Stella, the No-Handed Gut Rot, and—if you're lucky, and these pint-size pint-killers are still standing—the Moonshine. It's like the Moonwalk, except unattractive.

"Norm!"

"If you win, you go to bartending school. If I win, you go back to Madagascar."

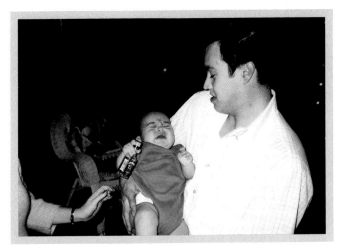

You never forget that first shot.

MY BAD PARENT

"We'll start you off easy, but you can't be doggy-paddling with just straight bourbon forever."

"One pitcher of vodka. Yeah, the family size."

"You know this ID's expired right? I'll take it this time, but make sure you get it renewed."

The important thing is not how cheap the weed is, but how . . . something, wut?

"Just a few moments of peace to take me away from all this sound and fury, signifying nothing."

Lunchtime in the Czech Republic.

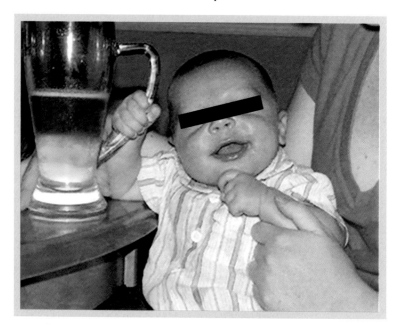

Now we know for SURE he's dead.

Six mint juleps into the morning, Julie's unwanted pregnancy finally redeemed itself as a thing of joy and wonder.

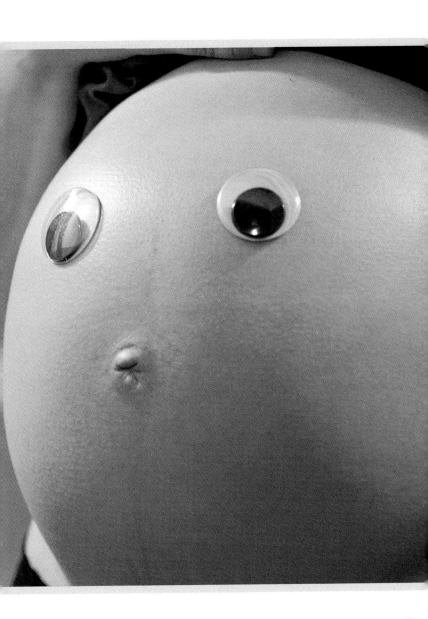

"Are you sure you're OK to give the toast?"

"And another thing . . ."

"So I says to the bitch . . ."

"Are you sure I only drank a 12-pack?"

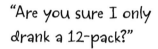

Scraping bottom for a designated driver.

9

PSA: JUST SAY NO
TO BATH SALTS

ECAUSE I CARE, AND DUE IN NO PART WHATSOEVER TO A RECENT COURT ORDER, I WOULD LIKE TO CLOSE THIS BOOK WITH A SPECIAL PUBLIC SERVICE ANNOUNCEMENT.

Bath salts, the wildly popular recreational drug for people who wish they were zombies, can make you extremely hungry. When you're on bath salts, the object of your gustatory desire starts with Doritos, graduates to pizza, and eventually culminates in a smiling Babe the pig. That's relatively harmless, but not everyone on bath salts stops with pork.

Remembering that pork is similar to human flesh (so I hear), your curiosity can quickly become a deadly force of hypnotic hunger that is devastating to those around you, including your cartoon-chicken-drumstick-shaped children.

Not that a baby sandwich doesn't sound really great right now (I'm in the program and recovering). And, let's be honest, there's nothing better on a summer day than a juicy crybaby hot off the backyard grill.

But that's wrong and bad; it's only the bath salts talking. Bad, Troy. Bad. So I'm not going to advocate such ghastly, delicious practices in this chapter. Be still, my grumbling stomach. Shhh.

Best part about this? He actually ENJOYS the basting phase.

Chipotle capitalizes on the
emerging zombie market.

The on-deck circle.

It's a BLT: baby, lettuce, and tomato.

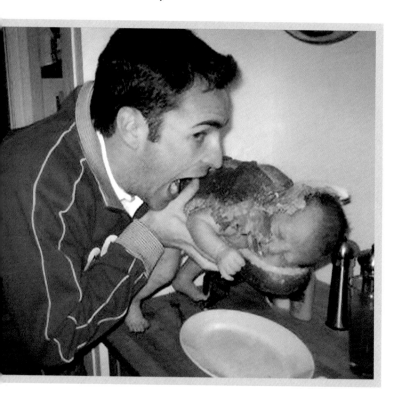

They've got tough skins, the little morsels!

Worst. Tanning booth.
Ever.

MY BAD PARENT

KIDS + KEGS = KIGS™

Second worst. Tanning booth. Ever.

Photographer of delicious babies Anne Geddes jumps the shark.

It looks innocent, but she always eats from the top down.

"Oh, don't cry. You get to have a nice basting, too! There, there.

PHOTO CREDITS

The photos on these pages are being published under the the Creative Commons License and were originally published by the following Flickr users:

page 13: izatrini_com, www.flickr.com/photos/izatrini /4495686746

page 23: izatrini_com, www.flickr.com/photos/izatrini /4495687024

page 38 (top): izatrini_com, www.flickr.com/photos/izatrini/4495048473

page 40: izatrini_com, www.flickr.com/photos/izatrini /4495686058

page 43: izatrini_com, www.flickr.com/photos/izatrini /4495048299

page 49: Jenny Oh, www.flickr.com/photos/jenny takesphotos/867561715

page 53: izatrini_com, www.flickr.com/photos/izatrini /4495048653

page 68: izatrini_com, www.flickr.com/photos/izatrini /4495686498

page 69: izatrini_com, www.flickr.com/photos/izatrini /4495047983

page 91: keeping it real, www.flickr.com/photos/fat_tony /3169816282

page 92: izatrini_com, www.flickr.com/photos/izatrini /4495048841

page 101: keeping it real, www.flickr.com/photos/fat_tony /3294681037

page 104: Natalie Steed, www.flickr.com/photos/bawdy_nan /4373072

page 120: izatrini_com, www.flickr.com/photos/izatrini /4495047751

ABOUT THE AUTHOR

TROY OSINOFF was raised by a pack of rabid Martians in Newer York, a thriving subterranean megalopolis famous for its complete lack of a decent sushi restaurant. He has no human children.